Cricut Mai

MW01128065

A Manual to help you Master your Cricut Maker 3, Cricut Design Space, and Innovative DIY Projects

Valerie D. Hering

Acknowledgments

Thank you Danny for your support. You rock!

Disclaimer

All the information contained in this book is purely for educational activities only. The writer does not assert the accuracy or wholesomeness of any info gotten from this book. The views contained within the pages of this material are those of the author in its entirety. The author/writer will not be held accountable or liable for any missing information, omissions or errors, damages, injuries, or any losses that may occur from the use of information gotten from this book.

Cricut 10 Books in 1 User Guide

The Essential Guide to Master your Cricut Crafting Skills with all Cricut Machines, Design Space, Profitable Project Ideas for Beginners, Materials & Tools with Easy Step-by-Step Instructions and FAQs

The ultimate must-have 10 in 1 Bundle to mastering Cricut Crafting from Beginner to Pro!

Have you been searching for that one guide to jumpstart your Cricut Crafting hobby or business? Do you want a well-researched guide to the latest Cricut devices on the market (Cricut Maker 3 and Cricut Explore 3) to make the most of your DIY skills?

I bet you answer yes to all the above questions! With your answers in the affirmative, I am glad to take you along on this exquisite journey into the amazing world of Cricut Crafts.

Time and time again, Cricut has sat on the throne of digital cutting machines, churning out machines of immeasurable quality that produce works of genius every time.

The challenge, however, lies in the inability of a lot of crafters to make the most of the latent and obvious potentials that these devices have in other for them to produce unique projects and make money from their works!

This 10-in-1 bundle is designed with you in mind in such a way to ensure that you properly glean every piece of information from guiding you from a beginner to a pro in the art of Cricut Crafts in no time.

It doesn't matter if you are an experienced hand or a greenhorn; the amazing wealth of knowledge, tips, FAQs, and hidden gems you will find within the pages of this book will go a long way in building your crafting skills.

You can seamlessly move from Cricut business ideas and Cricut Design Space to essential tools, how each Cricut machine works, to tons of amazing projects in between with a cup of coffee, and at the same time, you put all you are learning into practice. This bundle is all you will ever need as regards Cricut Crafting!

The 10 awesome books in this collection provide an endless stream of priceless information;

1. Cricut for Beginners
2. Cricut Machines
3. Cricut Model Comparisons
4. Cricut Tools and Accessories
5. Cricut Design Space
6. Cricut Project Ideas
7. Cricut Business Ideas
8. Cricut Common Problems and Tricks
9. Cricut Cheat Sheet
10. Cricut FAQs

With this all-encompassing guide, all your fears about crafting will dissipate!

Do you have questions about Cricut tools? Common troubleshooting problems? Confused about how to go about incorporating advanced tips and tricks into your projects? You are in the right place to have all your Cricut problems solved.

This book provides you with a well-detailed plan for starting a profitable business with your Cricut machine, simple ways of finding your way around the Cricut Design Software, and pointers to which tools are best used in different situations while crafting.

Here is a quick summary of the priceless nuggets you will be getting;

- The various types of Cricut machines available on the market and what features should inform your buying decisions.
- Moving around the Cricut Design Space Software and making the most of it.
- Designing and producing your first project, simple steps to guide you.
- Cricut Custom settings to use for different materials on the various Cricut devices.
- The vast array of Cricut tools and accessories and how to use them in your projects.
- Mini manuals for Cricut devices

- Profitable Cricut Project ideas and simple steps on setting up your Crafting business.

Bringing a warmth of beautiful, inspired Cricut art into your personal space, generating much-needed income through your Cricut craft, gifting loved ones thoughtful Cricut gifts during celebrations and festive periods, and much more are what this collection aims to achieve.

It's a no-brainer that you need to GRAB a copy now as you begin this beautiful journey into the world of Cricut.

https://www.amazon.com/dp/B0B4JS8KJ3

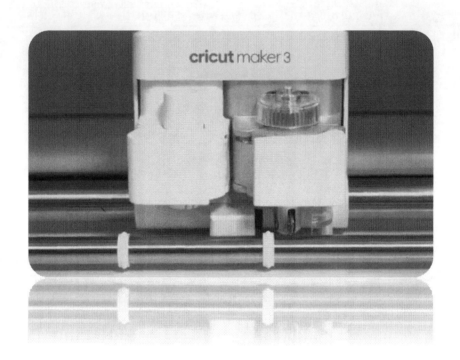

Contents

Chapter One

What is a Cricut Machine?

A Cricut is an electronic machine that can cut several items into various shapes and designs. While talking about a Cricut, you can think of it as a printer; you create your desired images or structures on your computer, phone, or iPad and then send them to the machine. But, rather than printing out your work as is observed in regular printers, the Cricut machine cuts out the predesigned pattern on the material fed into it e.g. paper, vinyl, fabric, cardstock, sticker paper, faux leather, craft foam. Some machines can even cut wood!

You can use a Cricut to cut anything you would ordinarily cut with scissors or an X-acto knife. A Cricut can carry out precision cutting than you can achieve manually. Devices like the Cricut are most times referred to as craft plotters or die-cutter machines.

There are presently three major Cricut machine lines available to crafters: Cricut Joy, Cricut Maker and the Cricut Explore. The Cricut Explore Air 2 is the mid-level option and the best-selling machine. However, the Maker is a step ahead of the Explore Air 2 and can cut a much wider variety of materials.

How does it work?

As said earlier, the Cricut cutting machine has similarities to a printer. But rather than print it on a paper, a specifically designed blade that is quite mobile carries out the cutting action on the desired materials.

When using the Cricut cutting machine, you first create any design of your choice in Cricut's design software. Then, the design is transmitted to the Cricut cutting machine via USB or Bluetooth. When the Cricut machine receives the data, it cuts them off using a small, precise blade. The Cricut machine typical usage can be explained in the following easy to follow steps:

- Plugin and open the machine.
- Plug the power adapter into your machine and then into an outlet. You can either use a USB or Bluetooth to connect. If you want to connect via USB, you will need to plug your USB cable in, while connecting via Bluetooth takes a longer step. First, you will have to click the open icon settings on the device of

choice,tap Bluetooth logo. You will need to turn it off if it is not currently active.

- Next, tap the wireless adapter or Cricut name to begin with the pairing process. After this has been done, press the button on the left side of the Cricut labeled "open "to open up the machine.
- Press the power button on the right side to turn the machine on.
- Log in to the Cricut design space.

Cricut Design Space is a cloud-based app that you use to design projects on your desktop, laptop, tablets, phone and communicate with your machine. Cricut Design Space contains over 400 fonts, 75,000 images and more than eight hundred readymade projects for you. If you're a brand-new user, it is advised that you use the New Machine Setup.

Choose a Make It Now Project to make or design your project.

Once you log in to Cricut Design Space, you can search for the "Make It Now" projects. While scrolling through, look for inspirations all around you before designing your project. You can either select one of your already existing projects or create a new project, whichever way you find easy for you.

- Once your project is ready, click "Make It" to inform your machine.
- Select on the Smart cell dial.
- Rotate your dial so that the dot on the pressure-setting dial faces the material you plan to cut. If your fabric isn't selected, choose "Custom" and select the material from the drop-down menu in Design Space.

Load your cutting mat

- Place your desired material on the cutting mat.
- Follow the instructions in Design Space for loading your cutting mat. When this is being done, be sure to press the flashing load button after placing your mat in the guides on the machine so that it loads appropriately.
- Press the Cricut button and allow the machine to go to work.
- Immediately after pressing "Go" in your design space, the Cricut button on your machine starts flashing. Press it to begin your project. If you need to change

anything, pens, blades, or mat, the design space will notify you.

- Remove and enjoy!

Once your project has finished cutting, writing, and scoring, Design Space and flashing lights on the machine will inform you to unload your cutting mat. Employ the same button you activated in loading the mat to also get it off the machine. After this has been done, you take your project off the mat and use it however you want.

The Cricut Maker 3

The Cricut Maker 3 quickly and rapidly cuts 299+ materials from the most delicate fabric and paper to the more challenging material like balsa wood, matboard, balsa wood, leather, and more. It is the most powerful, fastest, and most used Cricut device. The Cricut Maker 3 is pretty much faster than the machine that came before it. You can use it with the design space app forAndriod, iOS, Mac and Windows. It is also works well with the brand's all-new innovative materials for accurate cuts up to 12 feet in length without a machine mat.

There are also 13 tools available to cut, score, write, deboss, engrave, or add other decorative impacts with high professional-level accuracy.

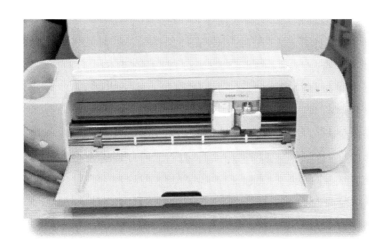

Parts of the machine

The Cricut Maker 3 constitutes of these parts:

- o The buttons (power, load and on load, start and pause button)
- o The Clamp
- o Silicon storage compartments
- o Tray
- o Ports (for power and USB cord)
- o Power adapter

o   Adaptive tool system

o   A slot

Features and how to use the Cricut Maker 3

The Cricut Maker 3 is sleeker and less cluttered in appearance.

Its features include:

o   Cuts over 290 different materials from wood to paper.

o   Cuts fabric and draw sewing marks.

o   Write and draw with several types of pens and markers.

o   Emboss, Score, perforate, deboss etc.

How to use a Cricut Maker 3

- Press the curved end of the power cord into the device and then insert the other end into a power source. The power plugin is located at the back of your device.
- Click the power button to power on your machine.

- Go to http://cricut.com/setup; this brings you to the correct place to download the design space app for your device.

- Link your Cricut to a computer either using a USB cord or Bluetooth.

- Tap on the new product setup, then, select the machine you want to set up (Maker 3).

- Follow the prompts in the design space, making sure that your Maker is plugged in and connected to your device, then click continue.

- Various images will be shown, then you select the one you will like to cut out.

- Inputthe Smart material of choice into the device, make sure it's underneath the white guides.

- Press the load arrow to load your material into the machine.

- Confirm that your blade is in your machine and press the flashing button to begin cutting.

- When the cutting is done, you press the unload button and take out the machine's cut.

- Your cut is ready to use!

What can I do with a Cricut machine?

There are a lot of things which you can do with the Cricut machine. And there is absolutely no way that I can mention all because the list goes on and on. Here are a few of the most popular projects to give you an insight into what the machine can do.

- Cut out attractive and exciting letters and shapes for your album decor.
- Make 3D animals for decoration.
- Make attractive custom, handmade cards for special occasions.
- Make vinyl stickers for your wall decal, car window, etc.
- Make a veneer clock.
- Make a front porch welcome sign.
- Make attractive monogram pillows.
- Make engraved bracelets.
- Make leather jackets
- Create custom-made Christmas ornaments.
- Create your window clings.
- Address an envelope.

These are just a few out of the many things which you can do with a Cricut machine. The list of items is too numerous to mention!

Chapter Two

Types and features of Cricut Machines

The Cricut cutting machine comes in different types with varying features, and they are:

Types

- Cricut Maker Machines(Cricut Maker 3)
- Cricut Explore Machines(Cricut Explore 3)
- Cricut Joy
- Heat Presses(EasyPress 2 Machines)
- EasyPress Mini (Mug Press)

Cricut Explore 3 vs. Cricut Maker 3

These are Cricut's next-generation cutting machines, bringing us new features and new materials to use with them. From a design perspective, almost nothing has changed in this new generation of Cricut machines. If you are accustomed to the Cricut machines, you'll immediately notice the curves and lines of both the Explore 3 and Maker

3. Here are the similarities and differences between latest Cricut machines (Cricut Explore 3 and Cricut Maker 3).

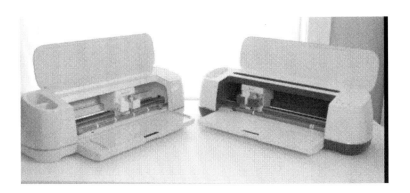

𝕾imilarities

- Both can cut materials faster (twice as quick as the previous cutting machines) and with more precision.
- Both can cut certain materials without a mat.
- Both can cut materials up to 12 feet long.
- Both can do a print and then cut on colored paper also white paper.
- Both have an optional hand holder feature, which helps to make it easier to cut from a roll.

Differences

Explore 3 is swapped with glossy and matte finishes to stay clean with little or no fingerprints, while on the Maker 3, there is a slight difference in color.

You can cut more materials with the Cricut Maker 3 than with the Cricut Explore 3. The Explore functions by dragging the blade across the material, while the Maker functions by actively positioning and turning the edge of the material as needed. It allows the Maker to cut more materials with ten times the force with accuracy and precision.

The Maker 3 is used for a considerable variety of productive projects, while Explore 3 is like the Maker but less expensive. The Cricut Maker 3 allows you to work on over 299 materials, including Smart Materials up to 12 feet long. It is faster than ever. While the Explore 3 takes smart materials up to 13 feet long, and it cuts twice as fast!

Final verdict

The various types of Cricut machines are unique and carry out projects that turn out beautifully. It is advised that anyone who wants to start up a crafting business should get either the Cricut Maker three or the Explore 3, as they are provided with all the features for versatility in performance and make your work easier and faster.

Chapter Three

How to set up your Cricut Machine

For iOS/Android

Setting up the Cricut Machine using iOS/Android

- Insert the power cable into the device and the power source then switch it on.

- Pair your iOS/Android device with the Cricut machine via Bluetooth.

- Download and install the Design Space app.

- Open the app, create or sign in with your Cricut ID.

- Click the menu icon and pick theApp Overview & Machine Setup.

- Go with the New Machine Setup option.

- Follow the on-screen prompts to complete the setup.

- You will know the setup is complete when you are prompted to go on with a test cut.

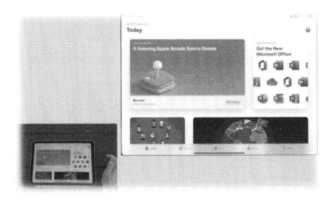

For Mac/Windows

Setting up the Cricut machine using mac/windows

- Plug in the Cricut device and switch it on.
- Link the Cricutto your PC with via Bluetooth or a USB cord.
- Type in design.cricut.com/setup in thePC browser.

- Follow the instructions shown on the screen to sign in or create your Cricut ID.
- When prompted, ensure that you download and then install the Cricut Design Space plugin.
- You will know that the setup is complete when you are prompted to produce your first project.

Using Bluetooth in Cricut Maker 3

You can wirelessly connect your Cricut Maker 3 via Bluetooth by following these steps:

- Ensure that your Cricut Maker 3 machine is properly switched on and within 11-16 feet radius of your PC.
- Bluetooth can connect most computers with ease. To check if your PC is Bluetooth enabled, click on the Start icon and pick the Device Manager option.
- If Bluetooth is listed, it means it can connect your computer to Bluetooth. However, sometimes the Bluetooth is not listed necessitating you to buy a Bluetooth Dongle to facilitate seamless linking of your device and PC.
- Shut down the Device Manager.
- Click the Start menu icon and choose Settings.

- Click the Devices option menu.

- Make sure that you have turned on the Bluetooth option and pair it to other devices.

- Select Bluetooth and wait for the computer to discover your Cricut machine. Select your device from the list.

- Suppose a PIN is requested, enter 0000, click on the connect icon.

Your PC is now successfully paired with your Cricut device.

Pairing the machine with a computer

Whichever Cricut it is you have in possession, pairing it to a computer is essential for any initial setup and cutting stage of any project. All the latest editions of Cricut machines have the capability to connect via Bluetooth, USB cable or through mobile devices.

Steps to be taken to pair your machine with a computer include:

o Plug in the machine and power it on.

o Link the Cricut device to your PC via Bluetooth or the USB cord.

o Enter design.cricut.com/setup into the PC browser.

o Download and install Design Space for Desktop.

o Go with the instructions on the screen to guide you in setting up your Cricut ID, setting up your device or signing in.

o You will confirm that the setup is complete when you are prompted to carry out a test cut.

Design Space can be used without it been directly linked to your PC at that point in time. It means you must not necessarily need the computer, as you can work on designs away from your device, and when you are ready to cut the projects, you connect the machine.

Unpairing

Steps required to unpair your machine from a computer include:

➤ Make sure that the Design Space for Desktop is closed. Not closing the app properly will result in it not been correctly uninstalled.

➤ Click on the Start image, then tap on the programs search icon.

➤ Pick on the option to add or remove programs. This will grant you access to the features and apps window.

➤ Search for "Cricut" using the search file.

> Go with the Design Space option, select the Uninstall button.

> Uninstall Cricut Design Space by confirming your action.

> The uninstallation process will be carried out to the end.

Resetting the Cricut Maker 3

For specific errors such as freezing, power problem, cutting issues, or anything out of the regular operation of the Cricut machine, a Hard Reset may be required. These reset procedures/steps help you start the troubleshooting process. They include:

> First, power the device without the presence of a cartridge. Then you turn all the grey dials to their lowest readings.

> After that, you will have to grip on the gold/green cylindrically shaped blade collection apparatus and employ it to move the carriage to the opposing end of the Cricut device. In the opening where the grey carriage car is located, a red button will be observed. Depress it and hold for a minimum of five

seconds.Then release it and move the grey carriage to its original position.

➢ This next step might sound weird but must be carried out to fix minor problems. You will have to roll the dials down and up three times for every dial.

➢ You'll then go and hit the "cut" button and then turn the machine off. Allow the machine to rest for a few minutes or even seconds, load a cartridge, turn it on and then try to work on a project and notice the difference!

➢ If the problems continue, it's advised that you seek help from any professional Cricut board repair company.

Finding the current version of Cricut Design Space

The design space changes as there are new features due to recent updates, which are released periodically. Nevertheless, the process of finding the version of your software remains the same.

Finding the current version via windows:

- Show the hidden icons by clicking on the arrow on the taskbar.
- Permit the cursor to linger over the Design Space image.
- Then, the new version will come up.

Finding the current version via Mac:

- Select the Cricut icon at the upper right corner of your screen.
- Select "About."
- A small window will appear, revealing the current version.

Finding the current version via iOS:

- Go to Design Space application, click to open it, and log in.
- Tap on the profile icon at the upper left hand side.
- You will see the version number at the lower part of the menu screen.

Finding the current version via Cricut Basics:

✓ Open Cricut Basics App.
✓ Open the menu on top-left.

✓ Then, the bottom left of the menu will show the version number.

Finding the current version via Android:

- Go to Design Space application open, and log in.
- Tap on the human-like image at the upper left side.
- The bottom left of the menu will show the latest version digits.

Finding the current firmware version of the machine

It is important to always have the latest iteration of the firmware to ensure a seamless operation. The directions listed here will guide you on updating and finding the latest releases of firmware for your device.

Cricut Explore and Cricut Maker

- Login to Design Space and confirm that your device is properly linked and functional.
- Click on the account menu in the top left area of Cricut Design Space, proceed to tap on "Update Firmware."

- Choose your device from the prompt options. The software will take a little while to recognize your device.
- Immediately your machine has been recognized, you will either receive a message that your firmware is up to date or you don't have any available updates.

Choosing material settings

These steps will help you figure out how to choose the most suitable setting to cut a particular material you choose to use for your project correctly. However, before I proceed to the steps, you must note that before rushing into cutting your material, it is advised that you perform a "test cut" with a small piece of fabric. It will ensure that the setting you have chosen cuts the material you are about to use for your project.

The steps to include:

- If Cricut Maker device is linked to your PC, the material settings appear as a sequence of tiles.
- If you see your material there, click or tap on the tile to select the setting.

- But, if these are not written down in your material list, you simply Click on "view all" or "tap all materials" so you can access the broad list of material settings.
- Since some options have been provided, you select a category, search for a different material, or scroll through the list using a desktop computer. Meanwhile, scroll through the list on the device or you can type in a phrase to look for your choice of material. As you type, the list refreshes with results.
- Scroll the provided list of options provided, choose your desired material to proceed.

Custom Cut Settings of the Cricut Machine

A "Custom" setting that is available on the Smart Set dial gives you the option of selecting already set and loaded custom material settings or you can as well create a personalized setting. If a situation arises that a material to be worked on is not available on the Smart Set Dial, move the dial to the custom option, go to the Cricut Design Space

and select Make It. You can select the material from the cut
preview screen if it is listed in the drop-dial menu.

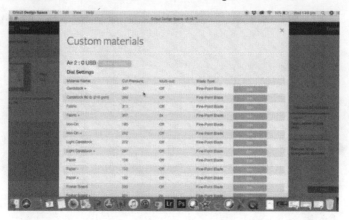

Creating custom material settings

Cricut Maker machines have the capability to cut a diverse range of materials. Hence, you have a lot of flexibility while working with various materials for your projects. Furthermore, you can choose from these pre-programmed settings or even create your own. How great is that!

If your material is not found in the Custom materials list, you can try the closest related settings or make your own. These steps are guides on how to create new material settings.

How to create a new custom material

Windows

- Open the Custom Materials screen. To do this, open the app menu and choose select Material Settings or "Manage Custom Materials," at the lower end of the screen while you are checking out projects to work on.

- Then, scroll to the bottom left of the list and click on "Add New Material."

- When you are about to save, make sure you specify the name of the material, then click on "Save."

- When you are done with saving the material, you can adjust:

- **Cut Pressure**

- **Multi-cut**; this is used for thick materials and this feature cuts a certain portion of an image several times to ensure that a clean cut is obtained.

- **Type of blade**; pick the blade type which is more suitable so that the Cricut Design Space will be able to direct you adequately.

- When the configuring is done, click on Save.

- Tap on the X icon at the upper right hand corner of the screen. By doing this, the new material will now show up when you search for it.

Note;

- In arranging the custom material settings, always make reference to the values for the material which is similar in quality to that which you are working on.

- Before you commence with a project, make sure you have carried out a number or trial cuts to ensure you get the desired results.

- With thicker or denser materials there might not be the need for more pressure but a multi-cut to cut through properly.

- Make sure you don't exceed the set thickness of the material.

- Flexible materials may be studier e.g. leather, however, they will be compacted when set beneath the roller bars thus the rubber rings will imprint on them. In order to avoid a situation like this, move the rubber rings out of the way and then proceed to set your material down.

Installing the Bluetooth adapter to the Cricut Machine

While installing your Bluetooth adapter, make sure to follow the steps listed below for a smooth connection. These steps include:

- Switch on the Device.
- Remove the cap from the Bluetooth Adapters.
- Insert the adapter into the Maker with the Cricut facing up.
- A blue light indicator comes up to show that the installation has been done the right way.

Chapter Four

Tools and Accessories Needed To Work with Cricut Maker 3

After getting your Cricut Maker ready, the next step is to decide which tools and accessories is a must-have for your machine.

Cutting Materials

Most people think you can only use a Cricut machine to cut paper or vinyl, but that is far from the truth as you can use the Cricut Maker to cut a variety of materials. A Cricut Maker can cut as deep as 2.4mm of any material.

Cardstock and paper: The Cricut Maker can perfectly cut paper and cardstock. Here is a list of different papers the Cricut Maker can cut: adhesive cardstock, cereal box, copy paper, flat cardboard, flocked cardstock, construction paper, freezer paper, flocked cardstock, flocked paper, foil poster board, foil embossed paper, poster board, notebook paper,

paper grocery bags, watercolor paper, white core cardstock, pearl cardstock, pearl paper, photographs, and many more.

Vinyl: This is one of the materials the Cricut Maker can cut. It is suitable for creating signs, stencils, etc. Examples of types of vinyl that the Cricut Maker can cut are adhesive vinyl, chalkboard vinyl, glossy vinyl, holographic vinyl, printable vinyl, stencil vinyl, metallic vinyl, etc.

Iron on: Iron-on vinyl is also known as heat transfer vinyl and can be used to decorate fabric materials like tote bags and t-shirts. Examples of iron-on vinyl are matte iron-on, printable iron-on, metallic iron-on, glitter iron-on, holographic sparkle iron-on, etc.

Fabrics and textiles: The Cricut Maker can also cut fabrics, but you need to add a stabilizer before cutting. On a Cricut Maker machine, you can make use of the rotary blade to cut the fabric. Examples of fabrics the Cricut Maker can cut includes; cotton fabric, burlap, flannel, canvas, denim, metallic leather, leather, silk, canvas, polyester, linen, etc.

Other materials: Apart from all the materials listed above, there are different materials the Cricut Maker machine can cut, and they include adhesive foil, corkboard, foil acetate, paint chips, vellum, wrapping paper, soda can, craft foam, balsa wood, tissue paper, etc. The Cricut Maker can significantly cut more materials because of the presence of the rotary and knife blade.

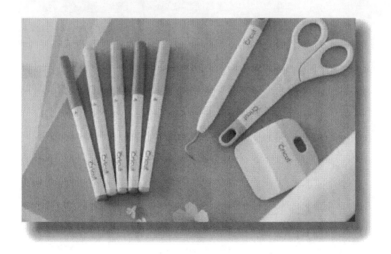

Accessories

Pens: Cricut pens come in a package of 5 or a box of 30. All the pens usually are permanent when dry apart from the glitter pen. They are to be used only on paper and non-coated materials because coated and glossy materials do not work with Cricut pens. It has so many colors and different finishes such as metallic, gel, etc. On the side of these pens is a letter at the end cap for easy identification of pens for each Cricut pen.

Cricut classifies their pens into five different categories, and under these categories are different colors with different options for you. They include Extra Fine (XF), Fine(F), Glitter Gel(GG), Gel(G), Marker(M), and Calligraphy(C).

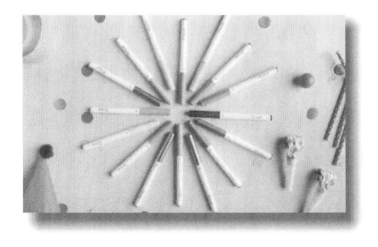

Selecting Pens

Cricut pens can be used for many things such as writing cards and gift cards, drawing on coloring pages, etc.

However, the most important function of the Cricut pen is to define your Cricut creation.

People who are familiar with Cricut know it to be mainly a cutting machine because they use it primarily for cutting. When will they ever know that it is also a writing and drawing machine? A fabric pen is also available when you want to mark a fabric cut on a Cricut maker. A Cricut machine goes beyond making T-shirts and cutting out images from scrapbooks. It can also copy handwritten notes easily.

One could create so many things with a Cricut machine while using markers and pens to write.

The good news is that all Cricut machines can use a pen, i.e., Cricut Maker, Cricut Joy, and Cricut Explore series machine. For the Cricut Maker and Cricut Explore, their pens are interchangeable and can be used for one another. But the Cricut Joy has a different set of smaller pens. So, you can't use the Cricut Joy pens on other Cricut machines and vice versa. Also, to differentiate them, written on the Cricut Joy pens is "Cricut Joy" while on other Cricut machine pens, "Cricut."

Here are frequently asked questions relating to the use of Cricut pens:

Can Cricut pens be used on fabric?

Well, you can use Cricut pens on fabric, but you'll have to take the precaution of making sure the pen does not bleed out before you begin to use it.

Can you use more than one Cricut pen color?

You can make use of so many colors on Cricut to make your design more captivating. Cricut has about 30 different colors to choose from their box set of colors. So you just have to simply make use of the colors you're willing to draw with, and the Cricut Design Space will guide you on what color you should load.

Can you use any marker available in your Cricut machine?

No, you can't. You can only make use of pens that have been specially designed by Cricut to avoid edge bleed when writing. Nevertheless, you can use special markers on the Cricut machines that look like the Cricut pens (their width should be similar).

The adapter is another exciting item when it comes to writing with Cricut pens. It will allow you to use Cricut pens made specifically for other Cricut machines, i.e., you can use the Cricut Joy pen on the Cricut Explore using an adapter.

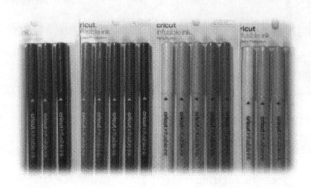

Cricut Pen and Marker Products

Selecting the right pens for your Cricut project can go a long way because it will determine what and how your project will turn out to be. Every Cricut project has a sure way to be customized when using different types of Cricut pens. For someone creating Cricut drawing projects, whatever pen you decide to choose will affect the project's outcome. There are numerous pen types for a user to choose from, and you can also mix and match the pen colors and styles to provide a unique design. So, how do you properly select the pens that you would use for your Cricut projects?

The most crucial tip to selecting the right Cricut pens for your project is testing them before use. Then, play with the pens, and notice how the pen draws because your personal preference of a particular pen also matters.

There are different Cricut pens and market products, such as the point size and type of finish. All pens are safe to use, do not contain any harmful chemicals, and are fixed when kept dry. The Cricut pens will bring forth whatever design the user has in mind, be it calligraphy tip, glitter, metallic, etc. There would always be a perfect pen for your project.

Here are the different types of Cricut pens you can use:

- o Extra fine point pen
- o Gold metallic
- o Precious metals (black, gold, and silver)
- o Glitter gel
- o Washable fabric paint
- o Ultimate fine point pen

Cricut produces a good number of pens and markers that users can use with their Cricut. They have been made so that they can be easily recognized by just looking at them. The barrels and end caps of the pens are designed to identify them.

Types of Cricut pens

Gel Pens: These pens have a rollerball in place of a felt tip. They have a white barrel with "G" inscribed at the end of the pen to denote "Gel." The ink of the Gel pens is very bold and thick.

Glitter Gel Pens: Just like the Gel pens, it has a rollerball. They have a clear barrel and sparkly lid with "G" or "GG," meaning "Glitter Gel" written on the end cap.

Fine Point Pens: These pens have a white barrel with "F" inscribed at the bottom to denote "fine." It comes in so many colors.

Extra Fine Point Pens: These are the more refined versions of Fine Point Pens. The older versions have a white barrel, and the new versions, a clear barrel. "XF" is inscribed at the bottom to represent "Extra Fine." Some older versions of Extra Fine Point Pens have only "F" written on them. It is perfect for writing on cards and gift tags.

Calligraphy: It has a grey barrel with "C" inscribed on end, meaning calligraphy. The tip of a calligraphy Cricut pen is angled, so it has to be set at a 45-degree angle when placed in the Cricut clamp. The Cricut calligraphy tip pens have a unique edge that appears chiseled. When using this type of pen on the Cricut machine, the weight lines will vary as the machine draws each line. These types of pens are especially good with fonts because the edge makes them look handwritten. Turning the pens in the pen holder will affect the outcome of the design, so at the beginning of your Cricut project, select the angle that you will use for the design.

1.0 Pens/Markers: This pen can be called a pen or a marker, depending on the product. They have thicker tips with different colors. They also come in metallic versions. They have an "M" inscribed at the end to represent "Marker." It is used for larger writing projects.

Fabric Marker: It was designed to work with the sewing patterns of the Cricut Maker. It has a white barrel and clear blue cap with an "M" inscribed at the bottom to represent "Marker."

Infusible Ink Pens: This is a new product from Cricut. The barrels and caps of these pens have a single color, with the barrel being white or clear, and the lid is colored. "F" is inscribed at the bottom to represent "Fine."

Infusible Ink Markers: These pens all have a single color (white or clear barrel, and colored cap). It has an "M" inscribed at the end to denote "Marker."

Point sizes of Cricut pens

1. Glitter Gel Pens: 0.8mm

2. Gel Pens: 1.0mm

3. Metallic Markers/Medium Point: 1.0mm

4. Fine Point Pens: 0.4mm

5. Extra Fine Point Pens: 0.3mm

6. Infusible Ink Fine Point Pens: 0.4mm

7. Infusible Ink Markers: 1.0mm

Pen tip size matters

The size of the design you choose for your Cricut project depends on the tip size of your Cricut pens. You should make small designs with a small point size, while larger designs would look different depending on what tip you decide to use, i.e., large point size or small point size.

If you want to draw at the edge of a cut line, choosing a small tip size might not bring out the design as you want it. Choosing a wider tip size will emphasize the design like it is supposed to. Practice with your pen sizes to know how well they draw at different sizes and with different fonts and designs.

Pen color vs. Sparkle

Cricut offers different colors of fine point pens for users to select. It becomes very important when drawing in colors of your choice, layering your draw lines with different colors, etc. Glitter and metallic pens are also available. These different pen types have different tips, and they would work better when used on specific designs than others. The paper used with different pens will also affect the outlook of your design. The glitter pens work better on medium detail and smooth paper; fine point pens work better on all types of paper except very-textured paper. Metallic pen-type works better with larger designs, cut edges, and any paper type. Glitter and metallic ink would come out beautifully on shinier surfaces because the ink would sit on top of the design instead of soaking in. But, the best tip is to plan your pens and designs and to play with your pens both manually and with your machine to feel what it would appear like on the design.

Combining pen types

It is the most fun part when it comes to using Cricut pens. Using different pen types will produce a unique mixture of drawing designs. Use different ink types on top of each other and pair different ink types to produce a fun handmade design.

There are alternatives to using a Cricut pen or marker. As mentioned earlier, you can make do with a third-party adapter, although there are still some pens that you can use without the third-party adapter. These pens should have the same size pen diameter, just like the Cricut pens. Some of the pens that you can use without the need for a third-party adapter include Pilot Precise V5 and BIC Marking Fine &Ultra Fine.

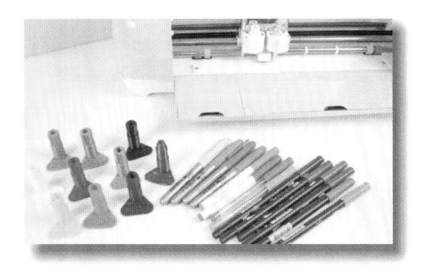

Paper trimmer: This can be used with materials with up to 12" wideness.

Scraper: It helps to scrape out excess pieces from your cutting mat after cutting.

XL scraper: This works better than the regular scraper when working on vinyl projects and transfer tape. It is more expansive and can cover more surface area when pressure is added.

Spatula: It is used to bring out cut images by lifting them from the mat.

Weeding tool: This is best used when cutting vinyl or iron-on. Like the term says, it helps remove unwanted pieces after cutting. It also helps pick up items with adhesive on it. You can also take advantage of the curved section of the hook, as you can use it to hold down projects when working on it.

Brayer: is good when it comes to vinyl and transfer tape, but what about thicker materials like leather, fabric, felt, etc. It applies even pressure and helps to load your mat correctly.

Tweezer: It is used for lifting and holding small pieces.

Mats

When starting, you would think one mat would do all the work needed to be done. There are four different types of mats, and it is advised to keep all four of them if you run across various projects. These four mats include strong grip, light grip, standard grip, and fabric grip.

The Cricut mats come in 12" x 12" and 12" x 24" and different degrees of strength. The four types of mats available on Cricut will let you cut pretty much anything.

The Blue LightGrip mat usually comes with new machines and can be used with regular materials like paper and cardstock. It also works with lightweight materials such as light paper.

The Blue StandardGrip mat comes in handy when cutting vinyl, iron-on, medium-weight cardstock, etc.

Purple StrongGrip mat works well with heavier materials, e.g., thick cardstock or anything that slips on the mat while cutting.

The Pink FabricGrip mat has a lightweight adhesive that prevents your materials from fraying once they are removed from the mat. In addition, the mat itself is strong enough to hold the pressure of the machine while it is cutting.

You can use the 12" x 24" cutting mats (StrongGrip, StandardGrip, and LightGrip) if you're working on long materials. The FabricGrip mat also has a 12" x 24" size. It comes in handy when cutting 12" x 24" paper or vinyl that usually comes in a roll.

Tip: Before you make use of a brand-new mat, make sure to stick it to your pants or shirt a couple of times. It is because new mats usually have a lot of stickiness, and it becomes impossible for you to get your project off the mat. It becomes easier to get projects off the mat once they become less sticky through the lint from your cloth. Not to worry, the mat will still have enough stickiness for future projects.

EasyPress mat: In as much as you like using towels or small ironing boards for your iron-on, the Easy Press mats do make the work a lot easier. It helps sends heat from the easy press back to your project so that your iron-on adheres above and below.

Specific blades and tools for Cricut Maker

3

The rotary blade and fine-point blades are usually included, but all the other blades are purchased separately.

Premium fine-point blade: This blade installed in your Cricut machine cuts most projects from paper to vinyl. They are durable and are known to be available on both the Maker and Explore machines.

Rotary blade: This comes with the Cricut Maker and can be used to cut any type of fabric (without a stabilizer behind). It can stay sharp for a long time, but when it needs to be replaced, replace it.

Knife blade: This blade allows you to cut thicker materials such as Chipboard, craft foam, balsa wood, basswood, etc. You can make do with a knife blade replacement kit when you notice that your cuts are not as crisp or clean like they used to be.

Scoring Wheel; the scoring wheel will give you a more profound and cleaner scoreline, unlike the scoring stylus. It has two-wheel tips; the single wheel tip used on regular materials and the double wheel tip used on thicker materials. The dual wheel tip will allow you to score coated paper without cracking if after it has been folded.

The double scoring wheel will allow you to create two parallel score lines.

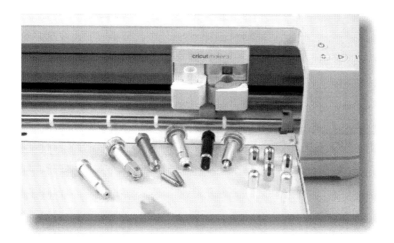

Scoring stylus: It can be used to add fold lines to your paper projects. This tool comes in handy when making something that you will have to fold up, e.g., a greeting card or anything three-dimensional. If you are making many cards, this little tool can save you from uneven folds.

Fine debossing tool: It lets you create clear and detailed debossed designs. The flexibility of the rolling ceramic ball will allow you to create your custom logos, patterns, etc., freely.

Engraving tool: It lets you make complicated dog tags that are engraved. It can be human or canine. You can also use it on jewelry, nameplates, etc.

Perforation blade: This blade creates even lines that give you clean tears without folding it first. You can use it to make homemade journals, shapes with curves, or any project involving a clean tear.

Wavy blade: The wavy blade gives you a creative wavy design at the edge of any material the Cricut maker can cut.

True control knife: It is easy to use and sharpen than most knives. It doesn't roll and is always stationary. The blades can be switched without coming in contact with it.

Extras

EasyPress: Traditionally, you need to use an iron or a commercial heat press to use the iron-on vinyl. Even if the Cricut EasyPress has the durability of a heat press and the convenience of an iron, it is more convenient to use due to its smaller sleeker size.

The Cricut EasyPress is designed to be a heat tool used for adding iron-on materials to your projects. You can use the EasyPress to place your design onto bags, shoes, hats, banners, etc.

The EasyPress has a more consistent pressure than a conventional iron, and through its digital control panel, you can adjust the temperature settings. It also has a timer that helps to prevent any guesswork with iron-on projects.

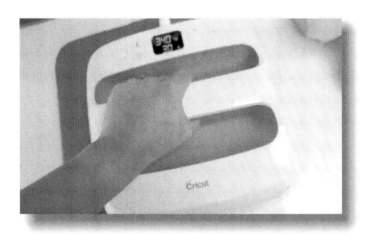

The Cricut EasyPress has even more features than the original EasyPress, and they include:

- ✓ The Cricut EasyPress can heat up very fast. It takes about 3 minutes for it to heat to about 400 degrees.
- ✓ It has three(3) sizes to fit projects that come in different sizes(from petite to XL). They include the 12 x 10, 9 x 9, 6 x 7, and the EasyPress mini.
- ✓ It stores your temperature and time settings when it is switched off. It becomes easier for individuals

working on a particular project for days or working on materials with the same heat settings.

✓ Its heat plate is more advanced than the original EasyPress with a +/- 5-degree heat variance.

✓ It comes with a rubber base to help protect your work surface.

Cricut machine tote: This tote will fit any Cricut cutting machine perfectly. The bag's features are carrying handles and a shoulder strap that you can remove, firm metallic flaps, and pockets at the side for storage of accessories. It has a luggage trolley strap located on the back to strap it to the Cricut rolling tote. It would allow it to glide firmly over the rolling bag handle like travelers normally do when traveling with their luggage. The most important feature is inside this tote with protective padding for the machine. This Cricut machine tote is distinctive from other bags because these bags only have fabric or a thin layer of foam as a protective cover for the machine. Meanwhile, the Cricut Machine tote uses the foam inserts that gear bags use when carrying high-level camera gear around.

Cricut rolling craft tote: The best and safest place for the Cricut machine tote is the Cricut rolling craft tote. Its features are spinner wheels and a telescoping handle to direct it. Outside the bag are pockets (two pockets are located at the side of the telescoping handle and one at each end of the bag). There are strong handles located at the end of the bag for easy lifting of the bag. The rolling tote and machine tote have a similar magnetic latch. Inside the rolling tote, there are exciting features such as the strap located inside the lid and is attached to the handle to keep the lid open when it is in use. Inside the open lid are two zip pouches joined together with the lid through hook and loop. There's also a laptop compartment located inside the bag to keep the laptop you will use with your Cricut Maker. There are also dividers located inside that are made with fine board materials. The contents of the Cricut rolling tote will remain organized no matter how little, or small they are inside the bag.

The bag's front flap opens completely to give complete access to the contents stored in the bag. The laptop compartment fits a medium-sized laptop. There is also room for a larger computer. The end compartments are made in a way to contain rolls of vinyl or iron-on. This tote is simply massive and can contain all the necessary accessories for your Cricut Maker.

Cricut EasyPress tote: This tote can package your Cricut EasyPress, mats, safety base, and small accessories that you will need to carry out your iron-on transfers. Heat-resistant materials protect it. Therefore, it protects your machine from bumps and indents. A shoulder strap and handle make it easier for you to carry the tote. The velcro strap directs the tote during travel. There are pockets located at the back and front to keep your iron-on and mat accessories organized.

Cricut BrightPad: When people hear of the Cricut cutting machine, the first thing that comes to mind is the vinyl cutter. One thing you would not hear about is how difficult it is to weed vinyl. It is the reason why Cricut has once again presented us with a good option, the Cricut BrightPad. They can also be called light pads.

The Cricut lightweight, BrightPad makes crafting a lot easier while reducing the strain on the eye at the same time. It comes in handy when in a dark room or at night. The portability of the BrightPad also says a lot, as it can fit into a carry-on bag. It sheds light on lines for tracing, cut lines for weeding, etc. People especially love it when they use it to weed iron-on. Normally, the lines of iron-on are hard to see, so the BrightPad serves as a big help then. The Cricut BrightPad comes with a nice box with space just underneath to store your power cord. It is advised to keep the original box safe as that is where you will be holding your Cricut BrightPad. Its power cord is long enough to let you relax on the couch as you work.

The BrightPad can work anywhere a power outlet is located. It also doesn't need a Cricut before you can operate it. You just have to switch on the BrightPad and adjust your level of brightness to your preference.

The Cricut BrightPad has five different brightness settings, allowing you to choose the suitable setting for your project.

As a result, people use their Cricut BrightPad to create almost anything like:

- Weeding glitter vinyl: Glitter vinyl is straightforward to weed, but individuals can weed glitter vinyl and glitter iron-on.
- Weeding everyday vinyl projects with too many words or complex designs: When weeding out designs with too many words, there is the possibility of there been challenges to eliminate those negative spaces.
- Tracing designs and making use of handmade hand-lettering cut styles: You can make use of the bright pad and iron-on to create special designs for your t-shirts or bags.
- Backlight for small projects: The BrightPad serves as a good lighting source when making jewelry.
- Tracing on fabric to produce an embroidery pattern: This is especially good for embroidering or cross-stitch people. With a BrightPad, you can make your custom embroidery patterns.

Chapter Five

Different blades for Different materials

The blades don't change as the blades you used for your Cricut Maker, and Explorer can also be used for your Cricut Maker three and Explore three as the case may be. Cricut has the most expansive range of blades which you can use on your machines. Choosing a blade for a particular material might be difficult. That's why I always advised that a "test cut" should be done to know what blade you need for what material and to achieve specific results. The blades come in different colors depending on their matching machine. When you walk into a store to get blades, be sure you get blades of the same color as the machine you have at home/ workplace. Here is a helpful guide to show which blades are available for which machines and the materials they can cut.

Fine point blade (comes with the Maker 3)

It is made to create intricate and minor cuts on work. The types of materials used for this blade shouldn't be complex but relatively lightweight- medium weight materials such as vinyl, poster board, cardstock and paper. These go with the Cricut Maker and Cricut Explore families. The color compatibility for this blade is either "Gold or silver."

The Deep point blade

This blade comes under the fine point blade family. The deep-point blade makes it able to carry out precision cuts on a diverse range of materials for your crafts. Compatible materials are thicker such as fabrics, foam sheets, stiffened felt, thick cardstock and magnets. This blade has a steeper blade angle at 60 degrees, whereas the other fine point blades are 45 degrees. It makes the blade more complicated and more efficient while cutting. The blade should be used in the appropriate deep point blade housing that comes along with the Cricut Maker. It can also be used with the Cricut Explore line of cutters.

The color compatibility for this blade is "Black."

Bonded fabric blade

The Cricut bonded fabric point blade is fabricated for putting precision cuts on your materials with your Cricut Explore and Cricut Maker devices. This blade is made to provide you with the functions of the fine point blade but in the color pink to match the FabricGrip (pink) mat. All

Cricut Maker and Cricut Explore machines can use this blade and housing. The materials that are most suitable for this blade are bonded fabrics and fabrics with an iron-on backing. The color compatibility for this blade is "Pink."

Rotary blade

The Cricut cutting rotatory blade is specifically designed for the Cricut Maker. It is compatible with the Cricut Maker Adaptive Tool System to cut almost any fabric quickly without the need for a back material. The rotatory blade can reduce fabric cutting time and cut out intricate patterns with precision. It comes packed with the Cricut Maker device. The rotatory blade only works with the Cricut maker because Cricut Rotary Blade requires the Adaptive Tool System limited to the Cricut Maker machine. The blade is compatible with fabrics that are delicate, soft, and thin materials such as; tissue paper and cork.

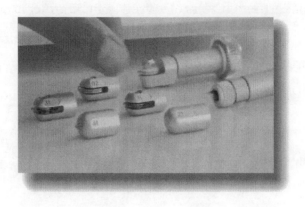

The blade is not advisable to be used for cuts smaller than three quarters of an inch or projects having too many complexities which may result in the blade tearing and scraping the material. It can only be used with the rotary blade housing and is only compatible with the Cricut Maker. It is advised that you keep the plastic cover that comes with the blade in place while cutting to prevent foreign materials from getting stuck in the gears.

Knife blade

The knife blade is made for slicing through thicker materials at a depth of 3/32" thickness. Therefore, it is excellent for using thicker materials to cut more intricate or detailed cuts in your designs.

Always move the white star wheels on the roller bar to the right when cutting thick materials with the Blade. It gives clearance for thicker material and ensures you don't end up with trails of marks on your finished work. Compatible materials are matboard, leather, craft foam, Cricut chipboard, balsa wood etc. The knife blade housing must help us with this blade.

Foil transfer tool

This tool is an excellent little accessory that permits you to add foiled details to your craft projects. It transfers and fuses colored foil accents onto the surface of your project. It's controlled through Design Space, to enable you make use of it in syncwith other accessories to engrave, perforate, deboss, score and cut foil materials for projects.

The tool comes with three tips; fine, medium, and bold. The main housing can easily swap these tips through a magnetic release system. The variety in thickness types are provided for other users and gives you the leeway to combine foiling for a number of works which is dependent on how pronounced or less pronounced the specifications are. This tool works on a wide range of thin materials. They include;

Cardstock, Kraft board, Printable vinyl, Photo paper, Poster board, Vellum, Faux leather.

𝔔𝔲𝔦𝔠𝔨 𝔖𝔴𝔞𝔭 𝔴𝔞𝔳𝔶 𝔟𝔩𝔞𝔡𝔢

It makes it possible to create decorative edges with your Cricut Maker machine. This blade offers a variety of techniques for your cuts and designs. The wavy blade creates a whimsical wavy cut and a decorative edge to your cuts. Materials that can be cut by the quick swap wavy blade include Matte, Crepe Paper. Craft Foam, Cotton (bonded and non-bonded), Copy-Paper, Construction Paper,

Cardstock, Adhesive-Backed Glitter, Adhesive Foil, Acetate (foil and regular).

This tremendous and specially sculpted stainless-steel blade is excellent for envelopes, scrapbook projects, gift tags and cards to impact more attractive qualities to the materials.

A Quick Swap housing is needed by the blade that is compatible with other Quick Swap blades. This blade can only be used with the Cricut Maker.

Quick swap Engraving tip

You can use this tip to engrave designs or words into materials to create beautiful work. It makes lasting impressions in a vast range of materials; also makes designs such as; individual texts, monograms, embellishments and flourishes.

Quick swap Deboss tip

Debossing Tip is another tip that can help create intricate design features and elegance with papercraft. It creates depressions in various materials to add dimension and flair to your projects without the need for a folder. For example, make tags, add flourish to gift boxes, monograms to thank you cards, wedding cards etc. It brings about an alluring effect on basswood, cardstock, foil, glitter paper, shimmer, coated paper and foil cardstock.

Quick swap Perforation blade

This is one of the latest additions to the collection of tools for the Cricut Maker. This blade is made to create perforation lines, giving room for neat tears without a requirement to fold, great for using with curves. It is a good candidate for journals, raffle tickets, tear-away pages and journals. Unfortunately, this blade type works only with the Cricut Maker and needs the Quick Swap housing.

The Quick swap Scoring wheels tip

This blade helps create more pronounced score lines and an impeccable finish on crafting materials such as cardstock and paper. They are employed in scoring sharp creases in thin and thick materials to form easy and simple folds in paper and card. Materials compatible with this tip are double scoring wheel, light cardstock and crepe paper. You require this for hefty materials such as cardboard and poster boards.The Cricut tip requires the Quick Swap housing and is only compatible with the Cricut Maker machine.

Changing the blade of the Cricut Machine

Cricut machine blades need to be changed on different occasions depending on the material you use with your machine. When you find out your cuts aren't as precise and as straightforward as you want them to be, then you know it's time to change your blade and get a more suitable one to give you a perfect finish. The steps provided below will assist you on how to change the blade in your Cricut without difficulty. They include:

Before we proceed, note that you will see two accessory compartments, Clamp A and Clamp B.

- Remove the entire blade housing from your Cricut machine.
- Steadily hold on to the top of the blade housing, it pushes out the blade. Then, you carefully pull out the blade and remove it from the housing.
- Due to the condition of your blade, it may just need a clean, or you may want to replace it entirely. Throw the faded blade away safely.
- Insert the blade in the compartment allowing the pointed end sticking out of the space (You can place the blade with or without a protective cover). Within

the compartment is a magnet that will attract and hold the blade inside. When it is positioned appropriately, you should barely see the tip of the blade. If not, you will know that you haven't correctly placed the blade and try to see what you did wrong while putting it in.

- Place the housing back into the B clamp in your Cricut machine.
- Close the lever of the clamp so that the housing is locked into place.

How to cut lightweight and heavyweight materials

These are steps in which you can cut a lightweight material (Fabric) on your Cricut Explore;

- Get your fabric which you might want to wash later, ready by pre-washing it.
- Cut your fabric to make sure it fits your Cricut mat. You can even go further to rip it along the grain, use a scissors or rotary cutter.
- Cut a little stabilizer of the same size as your material.
- Set the glittering adhesive side of the stabilizer on the inside part of the fabric. The glittering area typically consists of a rubber coating that can be fused to the fabric.
- Attach the stabilizer to the fabric with a pressing iron or an EasyPress. The temperature and length of time to press are based on your stabilizer material. If you use freezer paper, you can use it for 30 seconds at 350–385°F.
- Immediately the fabric has undergone proper bonding, set the fabric stabilizer side with the shiny

part facing up on the mat. A green standard grip mat or a pink fabric mat can be used to remove creases. Try and make sure to roll the Cricut application on the fabric for a stronger hold on your cutting mat.

These are steps in which you can cut a lightweight material (Fabric) on your Cricut Maker:

- Position your fabric right side down on a green StandardGrip mat or pink FabricGrip Mat to remove the creases.
- Set the Rotary Blade into the Cricut Maker.
- Put your Cricut Washable Fabric Pen into clamp A if you have any marking lines. It is entirely optional.
- Load your mat into your Cricut Maker.
- Select the material that best suits the setting for your fabric.
- Press the flashing button to begin your cut
- When the cutting of the fabric is done,take it out from the machine.

Forcutting heavyweight materials on your Cricut Explore:

- You can cut with a complete 12" x12" material.
- Use the Deep-Point Blade.
- Use a firm grip mat.

- Create a custom material in Design Space.
- Carefully place the mat into the machine, making sure that you place the mat straight and not slanted.
- You will see some markings from the roller wheels on the top of your material. A clean surface is integral to the final work so always flip the material over when cutting to prevent an imprint been left on the right side and affecting the quality of your work.

For cutting heavyweight materials on your Cricut Maker, the following steps and materials are required:

- 11" wide materials
- Deep-Point Blade
- Firm grip mat
- Custom material setting
- The White Star Wheels should be moved to the right hand side
- Reduce the material size to eleven inches.
- Ensure that you do not place the material too close to the left side of the mat. Rather, set it midway in-between the 0 and 1 area on the grid.
- Do not forget to alter the cuts in the mat preview to make sure that they appear on the project.

- Gently set the mat into the Cricut device and be sure to put it straight and not slanted.

How to Design, Clean and Materials that can be used

How to make your design using Cricut Maker

- Go to your Cricut design space.
- Click on the "Text" in the left corner of the space.
- Type out the words which you want to design.
- Note; if you want the font of the text to change, you move your cursor to the top left corner of the page, click on the font, and select the style you'll like to use.
- Zoom in the text a little bit. You'll notice the spaces between each letters. To correct this; click to move your cursor to the top of your screen and click on "Letter space," By clicking on the arrow facing downward, each letter comes close to each other.
- Attach the letters, click and drag the cursor over the entire text, move your cursor towards the bottom right corner and click on "weld."

- Then adjust the size of your decal to fit the material you'd like to place it on.
- Move to the top right corner and click on "Make it."
- Place your holographic vinyl on your mat and load your mat into the machine and start cutting.
- After cutting, unload and remove your mat. Make sure to remove the excesses for a clean finish.
- Now your decal is ready to be placed on whatever material or surface you want, e.g., wood sign.

How to clean the Cricut Maker

A dirty cutting machine can negatively impact on its cutting effectiveness. The machine should be cleaned as often as possible. Once you know how to clean your Cricut device, you can keep it in good condition and get the most out of it. You would not want to go about looking to repair your machine when you could have just cleaned it to prevent damage and rust. Here are the cleaning supplies we find most helpful.

- Cleaning kit
- Canned air
- Baby wipes
- Appropriate cleaning liquid

- A roll of paper towels and a few microfiber cloths.

Steps that must be followed while cleaning your Cricut Maker machine

- Make sure to turn off your device and unplug it before you start cleaning. It is the most crucial step as safety is important.

To clean the inside of the machine

o Open your machine and open the clamps as trays.

o Remove all the blades placed in the housing.

o Using the canned air (in moderation), to clean out your Cricut.

o Go around your storage trays, caddies, and clamps and clean properly.

o Wipe all areas that you can observe with a wipe.

o Move the stars all the way over to one side.

o Use a brush to clean under the trays and the rod properly.

o Move the blade carriage over just a bit and clean under that as well. Again, this should be done carefully in order not to mess up the machine.

o Go back in with a baby wipe to clean it thoroughly.

o Wipe the front row with your baby wipe but leave the back rod alone (the grease is important for easy movement).

Cleaning of the clamps

➤ The round bristle brush should be used for cleaning out each of the clamps.
➤ The Cricut pen adaptor can also be cleaned with the round bristle brush.
➤ Clean the whole machine one more time using the baby wipe taking note of the storage trays.
➤ Once you are done cleaning the Cricut Maker with the baby wipe, allow for proper drying before using a microfiber piece of cloth.

Cleaning the rear rod

o This part does not require a thorough cleaning because of the grease on the rod's back. Here, we use a brush to remove bits of debris found on the rod gently. Most of this debris is collected grease, so we then brush along the rod from where we have removed the debris to redistribute some grease.

- Carefully use a baby wipe to dab away any of the greases that end up on the machine around the rod.
- At the very back behind the back rod, check if you can see any debris present. If there are, you can blow that out with canned air. Once you are done, and your machine is looking clean and shiny, you can do one last clean-over with the canned air. Shift the star wheels back to the original positions, then close up your machine.

Cleaning the outside of your Cricut machine

- A paper towel with some appropriate cleaner is effective in cleaning the exterior part of the Cricut.
- Ensure that you do not saturate the paper towel and be extra cautious cleaning around the buttons. You don't want any moisture to get inside the button area and create a huge problem.
- If you see any trail of dirt on the outside of the machine that can't be easily gotten rid of with the wipes, spray a little cleaner onto a paper towel and use that to spot clean.

- To clean out the tool caddy, use the spatula end of the tool and a baby wipe to get right down inside it. Let it dry or dry it off with a paper towel.
- Use your microfiber cloth to clean the whole machine to remove any leftover residue.
- Use the canned air around any of the cracks and crevices in the machine.

Chapter Six

How to Design on Cricut Maker

The Cricut design space will let you upload and cut your images. It simplifies the whole process of customizing any craft of your choice. Design space is the best place for you to touch up and organize your creations. In addition, this space allows you to upload your fonts and images and make use of Cricut's premium images and fonts through Cricut access, individual purchases, etc.

Making use of Sure Cuts

Sure Cuts A Lot is a popular software created as far back as 2008 that helps users cut any shape of their choice with their electronic cutting machines.

Sure Cuts A Lot is the main deal because it is not only compatible with Cricut but with other cutting machines as well e.g., silhouette. Moreover, you can use its editing and drawing tools and free fonts to produce your designs.

Features of Sure Cut

1. **Metric units**: For individuals who like working with the metric unit, the Sure Cuts have metric units in cm, mm, and inches, unlike other competitors displayed in inches.

2. **Cut stencils**: The stencil bridge function of Sure Cuts allows you to connect shapes outside the area.

3. **Variety of plugins**: the Sure Cuts allow plugins for more than 30 cutters, so it doesn't matter the model or make of blade you're using.

4. **Versions**: The Sure Cut has both the PC and Mac versions of the software.

5. **User face**: The user face of Sure Cuts is customizable and can be changed to the user's preferences whenever they want.

Using Design Space

Investing in a Cricut would not be very productive if you do not learn how to use the design space because it will be almost impossible for you to cut any project. The Cricut Design Space is the best for individuals who are just starting to know about Cricut. People unfamiliar with Photoshop will find out that the Cricut design space is quite easy to use and understand. If you want something exclusive, you will have to create your designs or join the Cricut access membership.

When you first log into your design space account, the first place or page you see is the canvas, and this is where you begin or edit a new project. The canvas area of the design space is where all editing is done before they are finally cut.

The canvas is made up of four sections and four colors:

- o Canvas area(green)
- o Right panel(purple): Layers panel
- o Left panel(blue): Insert area
- o Top panel(yellow): Editing area

Top panel Cricut design space

It is used for editing and organizing elements on the canvas area. For example, you can choose the type of font you would like to use, change the size, align designs, etc.

The top panel is divided into two sub-panels. The first sub-panel allows you to save, name, and then cut your projects. The second sub-panel will enable you to operate and edit things on the canvas area.

Sub-panel 1

It allows you to move from your canvas to your profile, projects and finally sends your complete projects for cutting.

- ## Toggle menu

When you click on this button, a whole new menu pops up. This menu is an interesting one, but it is not part of the canvas. From the toggle menu, you can navigate to your profile and change your photo. You can do other important things from this menu, such as updating the firmware/software of your device, calibrating your machine, blades, etc. From here, you can also manage your account details and your subscription to Cricut.

- ## Access

In this menu, explore all the options so you can have an idea of all that the Cricut design space has to offer you.

Note: The settings option lets you adjust the visibility and measurement of the canvas.

- ## Project name

All the projects naturally have an "untitled" title. A project can only be named from the canvas area after you have inserted at least one element, such as images or shapes.

When you click on this option, it will take you to your library to find your past projects. It is good because you might want to edit a one-time project by re-cutting it. Also, it means that you will not need to recreate the exact project so many times.

- 𝔖𝔞𝔳𝔢

This option will only show up after you have inserted at least one element in your canvas area. It is advised that you save your projects as you proceed; although the project is usually saved to the cloud, if your browser crashes, the project also crashes.

- 𝔐𝔞𝔠𝔥𝔦𝔫𝔢

This option depends on the type of machine you are using. First, indicate if it is the Cricut Joy, Cricut Maker, or Cricut Explore machine. It is an important detail because the Cricut Maker machine has options limited to that machine.

It means that if you're using a Maker machine and you turn on the machine options for the Cricut Explore, you won't see the available options for the Cricut Maker.

- Make it

After you have finished uploading your files and ready for them to be cut, click on Make it. From here, you can increase the number of projects you want to cut. It comes in especially handy when you want to create more than one cut.

Sub-panel 2

This sub-panel is as essential as the first as it will help you arrange and organize fonts and images on the canvas area.

- Undo and redo

Naturally, as humans, we make mistakes, and these buttons better help us understand that. For example, you click on undo when you make a mistake or click on something you shouldn't have and click on redo when you mistakenly change something that wasn't supposed to be changed.

- Operation

This option is like a guide to the tools and blades it is going to use. Remember the machine option from sub-panel 1? It depends on the option you have clicked there that your operation will act on. Listed below are the operations that can be carried out;

Not all options are available on the different Cricut machines, but the Cricut Maker has all options available.

Basic cut: When you upload your image (excluding JPEG and PNG) to the canvas area, "Basic cut" is the default operation that all the elements in your canvas will have. When you click on Make it, your Maker machine will cut the designs. When you select the "Basic cut" option, you can change each layer's color, which will serve as the materials used when you cut your project.

Cut-Wave: Instead of using the rotary or fine point blades to cut out straight lines, this tool will produce wavy effects on your final cuts. Coming up with curved lines in design space is complex, so this particular tool will make it easier for you to make curved lines.

Cut-Perf: The perforation blade helps to bring out clear and crisp tear effects. It will help you cut your materials in trim and even lines. You can typically see it on coupons, raffle tickets, etc.

101

Draw–Pen: You can not only create simple designs but also write on them. For people who like to write on their designs, this tool is recommended. When you agree to this operation, you will be asked to choose from the Cricut pens available. When you pick a particular design, the layers on the canvas area will outline with the Cricut pen color you have chosen.

With this tool, when you click on "Make it," it will write or draw instead of cut. Keep in mind that this option will not do the work of coloring your designs.

Draw–Foil: This is the newest tool in Cricut, and it lets you make attractive foil finishes on your projects using the Cricut foil transfer kit. This option has three other options for you to choose from: the fine, medium, or bold finishes, depending on your preference.

Draw–Score: Score is a better option to the scoring line that you can find in the left panel of the canvas area. When you select this option to a layer, the designs will appear to be dashed or scored. It means when you click on "Make it," instead of your designs to be cut, the tool will score it. These types of projects require the scoring stylus or the scoring wheel.

Draw–Engrave: This option allows you to engrave different types of materials available.

Draw–Deboss: The debossing tip lets you create unique concepts for your designs by customizing them.

Standard (Print then cut): This option is used for printing and patterns. Print is one of the best features offered by Cricut because it lets you print your design, then cut. If the print option has been assigned, when you click on "Make it," you'll first send your files to a printer, then let Cricut do the rest of the work. Another feature of the print option is patterns. It allows you to add a pattern to any kind of layer. You either make use of Cricut's choices of pattern, or you upload your own.

Select all: When you want to move all the elements located in your canvas, you can easily select all of them instead of forcing them one after the other.

Edit: This option lets you cut, copy, and paste elements from the canvas. In the edit icon is a drop-down menu. The cut and copy option show when you have selected one or more elements from the canvas area, the paste option shows when you copy or cut a piece from the canvas.

Offset: This tool allows you to create a proportional outline inside a text, image, shapes, and outside. The tool becomes essential when making stickers or anything that you want to stand out.

Distance: This will determine the size of the offset. The maximum length that you can use is 1 inch in both directions. When moved to the left, an inline is created, and to the right, an outline is completed.

Corner: There are two options to choose from; round corner and square corner.

Weld offsets: If you want your design to have a single outline, check the "weld offsets" box, and if you wish for the method of a multi-layer design, uncheck the box.

Align: If you are familiar with other graphic design programs, you will know how to use this menu. The menu allows you to align your designs and is usually activated when two or more elements have been selected. Here are some align functions: align left, center horizontal, align top, center vertically, align right, center, and align bottom. The distribute option allows for proper spacing between elements. For it to be activated, you must have chosen at least three or more parts. There are two "Distribute" functions, and they distribute vertically and distribute horizontally.

Arrange: When working with more than one design or image, any new creation added to the canvas will appear in front. However, some elements are expected to be at the back, while some at the front. The arrange option lets you organize it efficiently. Some of the options include sending to the back, sending to the front, moving backward, and moving forward.

Flip: This option allows you to reflect your designs, and it has two options: flip vertical and flip horizontal.

Size: Everything you do in the design space always has a size. This option allows you to adjust the size of an item.

Rotate: Rotating an element can be done from the canvas area, but when you need to turn some designs to specific angles, this option works just fine.

Position: This box would show you the exact place your items are on the canvas area.

Font: This option lets you select the font of choice when you click on it.

Style: When your font has been chosen, it depends on you to change the font style. Some options include bold, italic, bold italic, and regular, which happens to be the default setting.

How to download

- Click on the Google Play icon on your device's home screen to open up the app.
- Search for Cricut Design Space in the search box.
- Click on the Install button to download and install the app on your mobile phone.

Cricut Design space top menu

New: This option opens a new project or a blank canvas for you. The functions listed in the new button are Save, replace, and cancel.

Templates: This serves as a guide to your design in your canvas area. When the "Template" tab is clicked on, a new page appears on your blank canvas, and here, you will find many types of templates made up of common items.

𝕻𝖗𝖔𝖏𝖊𝖈𝖙𝖘: This tab acts as a guide for any project. The "All Categories" is the default of the tab. You can choose different categories from the drop-down menu located at the top side of the screen.

𝕴𝖒𝖆𝖌𝖊𝖘: Here, there are many types of images available. It is a fascinating function.

𝕿𝖊𝖝𝖙: When you click on the text button, a text box pops up on your canvas area. Click inside the box, and type in your text.

𝕾𝖍𝖆𝖕𝖊𝖘: Here, you will find the scoreline. Choose one of the shapes displayed, and once your project begins, you can manipulate that shape into what you want it to be.

𝖀𝖕𝖑𝖔𝖆𝖉: You make use of this button when you want to upload anything from your files.

𝖀𝖕𝖑𝖔𝖆𝖉𝖎𝖓𝖌 𝖎𝖒𝖆𝖌𝖊𝖘 𝖙𝖔 𝕯𝖊𝖘𝖎𝖌𝖓 𝕾𝖕𝖆𝖈𝖊

Here, you can upload images from your files. The two images available are the vector and basic images. They include .jpg, .png, .svg, .gif, .dxf, and .bmp. While uploading images, you can remove parts of the images that you do not want to cut.

Spacing of letters

Usually, some fonts have a wide gap between each other, and this option will allow you to reduce the space quickly between these letters.

It falls under the right panel of the canvas area.

How to weld

Sometimes when you write text, the writing might not come out as you want it, and the letters might be too far apart. There is an option to weld this kind of text.

- Highlight your text and click on the Letter space located at the top of the screen to bring the letters close enough to each other.
- Ungroup your text, and highlight again by clicking on "ungroup," which you will find at the top right corner under "layers."
- Manually move the letters so that they overlap each other.
- Highlight all the letters and regroup them by clicking on "regroup," located at the top right corner under "layers."
- Click on Weld at the bottom right-hand side of the screen.

How to Slice

- Drop two shapes from the shapes button onto the canvas area.

- Overlap the shapes by placing one of the shapes on the other, select them, and click on Slice.

- After slicing, three layers are created: The shape you planned to cut out of the more prominent form, a copy of the form you wanted to slice out, and the last layer being the new design you wanted to create, which is a design with a cut-out of the image you wanted to slice out.

The same goes for text.

How to flatten

- Open the practice file in the design space.

- Select a word and drag it on top of the label shape.

- To print out the label and word to come out as one image, use the flatten tool. Flatten the label.

- Cut the Flatten layer to remove the interior cut lines.

- Click on "Make it" to make the image appear as a print, then Cut It image.

- Click on Continue.

How to attach

- Open the practice file in the design space.

- Position the text where you want it to be in the final project.

- Select all the teal images.

- Once all teal images have been selected, the Attach tool located at the bottom of the Layers panel shows up.

- Click on Attach to attach the layers which you have selected.

- Select the two yellow text layers and click on Attach again.

- Click on "Make it."

How to group/ungroup

This option helps you group layers, especially when you have different layers that make a design whole. By grouping these layers, you make sure that everything stays in place when moving around the canvas.

111

Ungroup allows you to ungroup the layers you formerly grouped on the canvas area. You can use the option when you want to edit a layer or element from the group.

How to delete/duplicate

The duplicate option allows you to duplicate any layer or design that has been selected on the canvas area.

The delete option will delete any elements that have been selected on the canvas area.

How to color sync

The color sync option allows you to sync all the colors in your project to cut on the same material.

Open the color sync panel located at the right side of the window.

Drag and drop each text to the layer you plan to sync to the design space.

Getting Started with Text

How to add fonts

- Open your Cricut Design Space App on your phone or computer.
- To view the Cricut font library, create a New Project.
- Click on the Text icon located at the left side of the screen to begin.
- Click to begin, and type in any text of your choice.
- Select the text.
- Change the font, font space, curve, letter spacing, etc.
- Select the font drop-down. Here, we can select a new Cricut font.
- The font drop-down presents a list of fonts for you.
- The fonts here depend on two sources: the Cricut font library and your system fonts.
- To select a particular font, search for the font in the Search Fonts bar.

How to edit images in Cricut design space using the slice tool

Once you know how to slice in Cricut design space, you can create almost anything. The Slice tool is a tool found in the design space that helps you alter shapes and images to create custom images. You can find the device in the bottom right-hand corner of the screen or when you right-click on options.

- Right-click to select the image.
- Click on Slice. It will slice your top image to the bottom image.

How to access special characters

To access special characters, first, add some regular text to your canvas area.

Note: Select a font that is known to have special characters in it.

- Bring out the "Character Map" on your computer.
- Select the font you will be using from the drop-down menu.
- Click on "Advanced view" to have access to the unique characters and glyphs.
- Scroll down till you see "Private use characters," then you click on it.
- The character map will display your unique characters. Select one of your choices.

114

- Highlight the letters in the "characters to copy" box, then copy it.
- Paste it in your design space over the letter you wish to replace.
- Make finishing touches to your text until you are satisfied with its look and the design is ready to be cut.

How to text curve

- After your text has been prepared, select the text and click on the Curve option located above the text.

- Click and remain on the handle.

- While you are holding on the left side of the mouse, drag the mouse left and right to adjust the diameter of curvature for the text.

- After your text has been curved, you can decide to adjust it. You can start by changing the letter spacing by using the arrows by the Letter spacing option.

- Rotate your text by clicking and dragging on the Rotate icon after the text has been selected.

- Prepare the font size, curve properties, and letter space to get your desired results.

How to make a stencil

When making a stencil, the most important thing to note is keeping an eye on the positive space and thinking of the negative space being created. For example, if you want to have a cutout for the Cricut machine that sticks together, you will need to avoid floating your design elements.

- Click on File, then New. It will direct you to a new design grid.

- Click on Insert images, and type in the image of your choice.

- Highlight the image, and click on Insert Image.

- Drag the image to the preferred size.

- Click on Add text located on the left menu(if you want to add text). To change the font, click on Edit located on the right menu, All Fonts, and select the font of your choice.

- Resize the text so that the image can contain it.

116

- Combine the image and text by clicking on Layers located on the right menu. Highlight the image and a line of the text. Click on Slice.

  𝕹𝖔𝖙𝖊: If your text comprises two or three lines, you click on the image again and the second text and Slice. You do this till you have entirely sliced all the lines of text in your image.

- After this, you will see that the text now has empty spaces in the image when you move the image. Delete the text boxes.

- Click on Select shape from the left menu, and select a square. Make sure that the square is more prominent than your image, so adjust till it is.

- Drag the image over the square. If your image goes behind the square, click on Arrange from the top menu and select Move Forward.

- Repeat the slice step mentioned above. Select two images from the Layers menu on the right side of the screen, and click on Slice. When the square is taken away, you will notice that the positive and negative of your design are left. The negative part of the design is the stencil.

- To cut the stencil, click on Go located in the top menu, and follow the remaining steps to cut your stencil successfully.

How to use Contour with text

- Open the practice file in the Cricut design space.

- In using the Contour feature, you need to select one layer(the image is usually a multi-layered image).

- Click on Contour at the bottom of the Layers panel. It will bring up the Hide Contour window.

- The Hide Contour window will show you all the cut lines that make up your image.

- The main window on the left displays actual shapes that are cut out of the material, which appears to be light grey, and the background color seems to be white.

- Click on cut lines to make them disappear until you have rightly covered all the important cutout details.

- When all the parts have been hidden, click on X located at the top right corner.

- With the cutouts out of the way, and you are left with a solid text having a teal shadow at its back.

- If you want to put back the cutout details, click on the main text layer. Tap on the Contour icon and click on the hidden cut lines to make them "reappear".

Chapter Seven

Vinyl for Cricut Projects

Vinyl tricks

Cricut can cut a wide variety of materials, so cut whatever type of vinyl you decide to use. Keep in mind that some types of vinyl are better than others, and certain types of vinyl suit other projects when used. There are two main types of vinyl: adhesive vinyl and heat transfer vinyl or HTV. Under the different types of vinyl are different kinds which are used for specific purposes and projects.

For HTVs, you would have to learn how to remove your carrier at the right time to avoid ruining your project.

Vinyl usually comes in 12" sheets, or you can buy it in rolls in different lengths. The best place that is advised to buy vinyl is online, as that is where you can find the best stuff. Look for an online company specializing only in vinyl as they would have the best quality for you.

Try to order your vinyl in rolls to save some money.

Using the Cricut Transfer Tape

The tape is used to transfer adhesive vinyl to your project. After you have cut and weeded your vinyl, place the transfer tape over your design. Let it relax using a squeegee. Then, take away the backing from the vinyl. It leaves your design on the tape. Next, lay it on your project and smoothen it down with a squeegee again. To let it rest on the project, add a bit of pressure by rubbing harder over your design area. Finally, peel the transfer tape, and your project will stick to your vinyl.

Types of vinyl to layer

- Oracle 651 permanent adhesive vinyl: This is the best type to use when you're putting it somewhere you want it to last on.

- Foil, glitter, holographic, and holographic sparkle iron-on.

- Sportflex iron-on

- Premium vinyl (permanent and removable)

- Vinyl on wall

You can customize your home with the vinyl wall decoration. Choose the color of the sticky-backed vinyl to correspond with the color of the wall where you want to place it.

Removable indoor vinyl is excellent for wall decals and anytime you want a provisional application on something.

Iron-on wall

A smooth surface is needed to add vinyl, but textured surface like walls can also work.

Make use of a transfer tape that is not too sticky. Note that people prefer the paper transfer tape to the clear or plastic transfer tapes. Rub transfer tape and vinyl to the wall using a sponge. On a flat surface, a flat scraper would work just fine to push the vinyl down.

Another method to try is by heating the vinyl with a hairdryer, and when it becomes warm, use a washcloth to press the vinyl down on the wall. Blast it with cold air before you remove the transfer tape. Remove the transfer tape slowly. Rub over the vinyl once again once it is placed on the wall.

Weeding iron-on vinyl

One step that comes with cutting and ironing iron-on vinyl is weeding it.

Weeding iron-on vinyl is the process of removing excess materials that you do not want on your project. You will use a weeder or weeding hook to do the work.

Before you begin to weed, when you cut out your design on iron-on vinyl, be sure to mirror it. You can mirror it in the Prepare Screen on the Cricut design space.

Applying iron-on vinyl

- Create a new design space project.
- Prepare your design for cutting.
- Cut out your design using your Cricut maker.
- Place the design on your craft.
- Once you have finished cutting the design, select the Unload/Load button to remove the mat from the device.

- Turn the mat to the other side and peel off the mat from the HTV. While doing this, keep the vinyl flat on the table to avoid it curling.
- Weed away the unwanted HTV with a weeding hook to get the needed design.

Adhesive vinyl

You can stick this kind of vinyl on materials like mugs, windows, or cars. There are two types of adhesive vinyl: permanent adhesive vinyl(the standard type is the Oracle which uses different numbers to represent the different vinyl types) and removable adhesive vinyl.

Heat transfer vinyl

It is also known as iron-on vinyl and can be applied onto clothing, tote bags, etc., using a heat press. The best HTV is Siser Easy Weed. This vinyl is easier to weed as it is thinner than other HTVs in the market.

Cling vinyl

Static cling is made from a thin vinyl film that can cling on various surfaces(the window cling is a static cling vinyl used on windows and mirrors). This type of vinyl does not have adhesive, so it is preferred for indoor use.

124

Design Space Software Secrets and the Design Space App

1. You can customize your designs using Weld, Contour, and Slice.

2. You can explore using your search box.

3. You can search by synonym as this will help provide all the possible images you will need.

4. Make use of free images and texts, especially when you're not ready to go on the Cricut Access subscription.

5. You can re-color quickly using the color sync tool.

6. You can manipulate patterns to fit your preference.

Chapter Eight

Cricut Projects

Customized Umbrella (Mickey Mouse Design)

Materials

Clear Umbrella

A pack of Cricut vinyl

Cricut Machine

Directions

o Fix the image on the canvas screen of the Cricut Design Space. Under the 'Create a Critter Cartridge,' you will see a balloon there. Use that one. You can remove the topmost layers by clicking on the eye-shaped icon that is located towards the right.

o Fix the shape you want to work with. Here, the impression of ears was added to the design with the aid of oblong circles.

o Highlight the three layers of images and then weld them together by clicking the icon on the right. After you at done with the initial one, you can make duplicates by working on the 'copy' principle. If necessary, you could resize the images. Remember that this project involves you introducing four vinyl stickers to the body of a transparent umbrella. Two of the stickers will be big, and the other two will be small. You can flip the images and also shift them about the canvas until they fit the page. Please get all the images into a box of 12 inches by 12 inches. This way, all of the images will still be on their part of the mat.

o Before you start cutting out the project, you need to make sure that the dial is pointing towards the vinyl compartment.

o At the bottom of the page, you will see a 'Go' icon towards the right-hand side. Click on it. Then, introduce the vinyl into the cutting machine with its face up. Do this process again for every color you use.

o Weed out the excess vinyl.

o Cut out the balloons you need for your project. This way, you would be able to focus on what patterns to make quickly. When attaching these cuttings to the transparent umbrella, do not use tapes. Tapes only end up leaving the marks of glue on the surface of the umbrella. Also, before you fix anything to the surface of the umbrella, you have to make sure that you have thoroughly cleaned the work surface.

o To fix the vinyl, peel the protective sheet that covers the gluey part of it. Then, you can proceed to fix the vinyl to the inner part of the umbrella. This technique will ensure that the vinyl stands the test of time.

o You can fix the vinyl anyhow you want. You can cause some to overlap a bit, leave some as straight, or even bend some through a distance.

o After fixing the vinyl, you will have to leave the umbrella open for some days. This technique will ensure that the vinyl has been permanently fixed to the body of the umbrella.

Dress Embellishments

Materials

Cricut machine

Iron-on vinyl (HTV)

Iron/EasyPress

Dress

Directions

- Upload your image design onto the canvas screen of the Cricut Design Space application. Afterward, duplicate the images.

o Here, the shapes used for the project include swirls, giant stars, small stars, and a mickey mouse that will appear blended into the background.

o For this project, see that you select the Iron-on option and then the mirror image icon.

o Once you are done cutting out the shapes on the vinyl material, you will need to iron them on the fabric's surface.

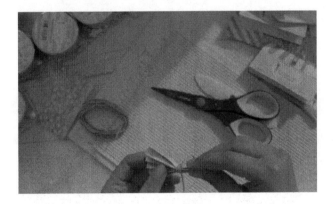

Floral Vinyl Wall Decals

Materials

Floral SVG file

Cricut device

Transfer tape

Weeder

Scrapper

Mat

Making Floral Vinyl

- ➢ Measure the width you want the images to contain. Then select the correct size you want the flowers to look like.

- ➢ Upload the SVG file to your Cricut design space. If you need to resize them, do that on the design space.

- ➢ Transfer the file to your Cricut machine. Put the removable indoor vinyl facing up.

- ➢ If there is excess vinyl, weed it out.

- ➢ Put the transfer tape on the front of the vinyl you had weeded with the scraper.

- ➢ Peel the back of the indoor vinyl.

> Place it on the wall gently and ensure you place it well.

> Then, peel the transfer tape away slowly and carefully. If some parts do not stick to the wall, scrape them with your scraper.

Acrylic Key Chains

Materials

Acrylic key chain

Adhesive Vinyl

Weeding tool

Cricut machine

Transfer Tape

SVG file

Directions

- Cut the SVG file using your Cricut machine, then resize depending on the size of the chain.

- Weed out the vinyl, and write any inscription you want on the blank space.

- Take it out of the machine using transfer tape; ensure peel off the blank thoroughly.

- Line your key chain up with the vinyl Design keyhole.

- Mount a slight pressure so that the design will stick to the chain firmly.

- Peel the transfer tape off.

- To complete this project, connect the hook with the key chain

- You can decide to seal it or not.

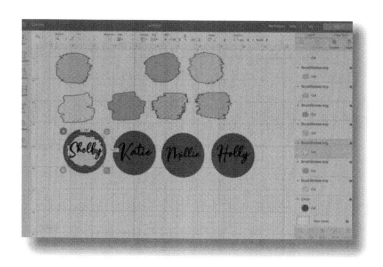

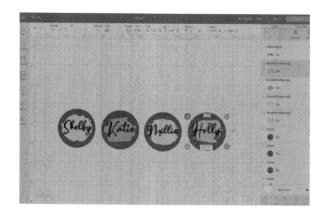

135

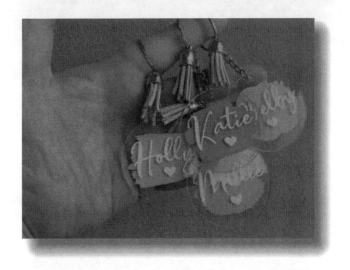

Wood Sign

Materials

Wood stain

Wood board

136

Cricut Device

Towels

Sandpaper

Transfer Tape

Saw

Directions

- Select the surface you want.

- Then cut the wood to the size of your choice.

- Paint or stain the color according to your choice and leave to dry.

- Use vinyl transfer tape to help place the letters in the right place.

- Use an acrylic product to seal up the rustic sign so it can last long.

Paper Flowers

Materials

Cricut machine

Cardstock

Cricut scoring tool

Wooden half circles (1.5)

Got glue

Yellow spray paint

Styrofoam round

Directions

- Load your cardstock to your Cricut mat.

- Use a scoring tool to form notches that you need in the petals; use the scraper tool to bend the cardstock so they can look active.

- Twirl the outsides a bit so the cardstock can bend.

- Cut the center of the paper flower with Styrofoam rounds into half to make it the middle of the flower.

- Use hot glue to glue the half wooden circles to the foam round tops.

- Spray the paper flower with yellow paint.

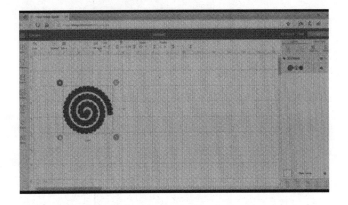

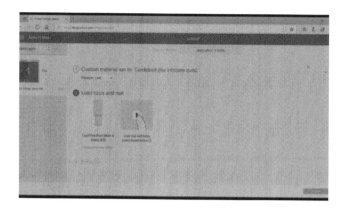

Birthday Cake Topper

Materials

Craft knife

Cardstock

Chipboard

Directions

- Create a design on the design space with the name of the celebrant.

- Cut it out with Cricut chipboard.

- Make the wheels cut rightly into the paper, then taper down the bottom of the chipboard or use a craft knife to cut.

- Then paint it and leave it to dry.

Flower Corsage

Materials

Cardstock of any color

Glue

Scissors

Ribbons

Pins

Free template

Directions

- Print out the template of your project on any cardstock of your color choice. Then, you can use your Cricut Maker to cut.

- Drizzle a little bit of water across the paper cuttings. This technique makes it easier for the paper material to be carved into different shapes.

- Glue the sheets together at the section where the leaves should meet. Then, please leave it to dry. Then, you can use cloth pins to fasten the ends together.

- You can color the leaves with watercolor or markers. This technique will add a unique vibrancy to your projects. Then, fix the petals and leaves together to make a flower. Leave the leaves to dry.

- For wrist corsages, you could cut out the band length that fits your wrist. Then, you can fix the flower's core to the band. You can gift out the flowers by adding some finishing touches like nylon wraps and keepsake boxes.

Leather Hair Accessories

Materials

Metallic leathers

Cricut felt

Adhesive

Headband

Chopstick

Hair clips

Cricut knife blade

Cricut Maker

Directions

- Upload the design in your Cricut design space. Resize to your taste.

- Put the leather on the Cricut mat. Ensure the purple mat is well placed so that the mat will stick to the leather.

- Transfer the design to the Cricut machine.

- Use a Cricut Maker to cut the designs.

- Take out the leather designs, then glue the pieces of flowers together with the adhesive.

- Include a button in the middle.

- Glue your flower to the headband.

- Fold your bow into two equal halves and glue it at the center. Repeat the process at the two sides. Hold them together using a pin.

- Glue the bow to your ribbon and hold it with a pin, then wrap a piece of rectangle felt around the middle of your bow and glue at the backside. Hold them together with a pin till they dry.

- Look for a chopstick that can pass through the accessory.

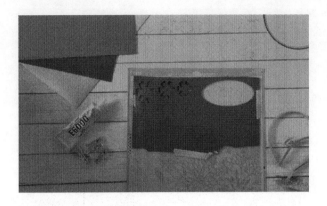

Leather Journal

Materials

Cricut Maker machine

Fine point blade

Cricut faux leather

Cricut Iron-On foil

Cricut EasyPress Mat

Cricut cutting mat

Cricut bright pad

Iron-On protective sheet

Glue

Directions

- Create a design on design space.

- Slide your mat in the machine and put your scoring wheel in its holder.

- Take out the scoring wheel and put a fine blade in its place. Do not take out the mat during the process.

- Put the Blade and click on the C button to cut the shape.

- Cut image on vinyl.

- Press the journal cover with EasyPress on your EasyPress mat, then cover it up using a protective sheet afterward; press it for about fifteen seconds.

- Leave the iron-on to cool down totally; peel the back of the carrier sheet.

- Afterwards cut a piece from the faux leather to cover the slots on your journal. Put some rubber cement at the backside of the cover and on topmost area of the cut. Do not put glue on the back piece in-between your slit.

- Leave to dry and cover it up with slits with small pieces.

- Afterward, apply rubber cement on the top of the book and the inside of your journal. Leave them to dry.

- Press the book on the cement of your leather. Put rubber cement in the book's backside and inside too.

- Do not put in between the scored lines. Leave the cement to dry. Press and line together.

- Press it well so that the book can stay in place.

- Your leather journal is ready for use. Now fold the top flap over and put a pen into the slit loop. Then clasp it.

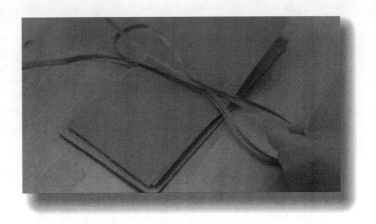

Curving Text for Tumblers

Materials

Cricut Maker

Cricut Scraper

Cricut Weeder

Cricut transfer tape

Holographic Vinyl

Permanent Vinyl

Plastic tumblers

Tip: Continuous layers of text cannot be used for tumblers because they are round. The roundness of a tumbler usually increases from the bottom to the top. So, consecutive layers of text will appear bent when fixed to the tumbler. The longer your texts are, the more bent they will appear on the tumbler. To avoid that issue, follow the procedures below.

- Click the 'template' icon and search for tumblers. This feature will bring you a lot of search results. Please choose any of them.

- Apply the template to your texts, layer by layer. This feature will add a curve effect to the text.

- You can only effect curves on single layers of text. Now, this needs you to be careful. You cannot have successive texts with the same diameter as the first one. There has to be a gradual decrease in each text's diameter. So you will need to plan out the diameter of each text layer. Your plan outline depends on the height of your tumbler and your designs.

- You can set the diameter of the first layer of text to fifty. Then, you can decrease the diameter by five inches as you go down. So, you have a diameter of forty-five and then forty.

- Once you finish cutting the vinyl, ornate it with holographic vinyl. Then, fix it to the surface of the tumbler. You will find out that even though the text is curved appears straight. That is the trick!

Note: If you are only washing with dishwashers, do not bother using the holographic vinyl. Stick with the permanent vinyl.

Glass Ornaments with Adhesives

Glass ornaments are ornate equipment you can use for interior decoration. To make them more beautiful, you can add vinyl cuts to the surfaces.

Materials

Glass ornaments

Adhesive Vinyl

Cricut Maker

Cricut transfer tapes

Hint: Do not go for too sticky tapes. If that is what you have, try to get rid of the glue. You can do this by sticking it again and again to surfaces like fabric. Using sticky surfaces can only lead to the color coating of the ornaments scraping off with the vinyl.

Directions

❖ After typing your text, reduce the size to something small. These glass ornaments are usually small and circular. This technique will prevent a case where you have to cut out important layers of text.

- ❖ Fix the Vinyl to the ornaments' surface and then press it with your thumbs directed outwards. Make sure you do not push too hard, though. These ornaments are made of glass; note that.

Cricut Infusible Ink Mousepad

Materials

Infusible ink transfer sheet

Mousepad for the sublimation

Butcher paper

White cardstock

Cricut Maker

EasyPress 2

Mat

Directions

- Cut the ink transfer sheet with your Cricut machine.

- Mirror the image before you cut it.

- Weed excesses with your fingers.

- Take out the lint from your mousepad.

- Preheat for about ten seconds.

- Leave the mousepad to cool off, then taper the design.

- Use Butcher paper to cover it and press it for about thirty seconds at 400°.

- Take out the transfer sheet when it is cool.

Dos and Don'ts of the Cricut Maker 3

Things to do while using a Cricut maker three include:

- ✓ Clean your machine before you begin cutting to prevent stains.

- ✓ Make sure that there's some free space around the Cricut so you can load mats in and out of the machine quickly.

- ✓ Place the Cricut on a long, flat surface for smooth cuts.

- ✓ Place your fine pointer blade properly before you commence cutting.

- ✓ Make sure that you have access to the internet to download and start using the Cricut design space app.

Things you should avoid while using a Cricut maker 3:

- - Do not use a dirty Cricut machine for your projects.

- - Do not connect your Cricut machine to a low powerhouse.

- Do not bang on your Cricut machine.

- Do not place your hands inside the machine while cutting.

- Do not use a spoilt or blunt blade to cut your materials.

- Do not place your Cricut machine on a rough surface while using it.

- Do not leave your machine powered on while not in use.

FAQs

How does the Cricut machine work?

This question is quickly answered by the starter project that usually comes with the machine to give you an idea of the machine's features.

Can I upload my images on Cricut?

Of course, yes, you can. It is not everybody that would want to subscribe to the Cricut access. Through the design space, you can upload any image to write or cut.

What materials can I cut with my Cricut?

The Cricut Maker can cut more materials than the other machines. This book mentions a lot of them.

Is it necessary to use cartridges with my Cricut?

No, it is not necessary. However, if you have cartridges from your old machine, you can use them on your new machine.

Conclusion

The Cricut Maker 3 cuts more than 300 materials from the thinnest to the thickest. It is compatible with 13 tools in total, i.e., cutting, scoring, writing, etc. It is good news for crafters because they have always wanted to do more as usual. The Cricut Maker 3 will allow them to be able to craft anything and everything.

Other Books by the Author

The Essential Bath Bomb Beginner's Manual: A Step-by-Step Guide to Making 95 Organic Homemade Bath Bombs, Body Scrubs, Bath Salts Beauty Recipes for a Healthy Skin

https://tinyurl.com/7zd63bdp

DIY Homemade Disinfectant Wipes and Sprays with Natural Recipes: A Practical Step-by-Step Guide to making Antiviral and Antibacterial Surface and Hand Wipes and Disinfectant Solutions

https://tinyurl.com/k3m8pr2f

Cricut Explore 3 Guide for Beginners: Master your Cricut Explore 3, Cricut Design Space, Troubleshooting, Essential Tips, Start a Profitable Business ... and Amazing Project Ideas (Cricut Mastery)

https://www.amazon.com/dp/B09CRNHXLX

About the Author

Valerie has several years of experience in the hygiene industry, hobbies and crafts for adults and children alike; the home crafting of skincare products for the whole family. Her books feature how-to guides, pictures, invaluable hints, and so much more. She has taught her craft at several schools, conferences, and workshops, which allows the participants to appreciate and hone their skills with firsthand experience.

She is married with two lovely girls and lives in Austin, Texas.

Made in the USA
Coppell, TX
14 March 2024

30100246R10090